I Love Your Brown

Daneýa L. Jacobs and Atiya Chase, M.Ed

Archway Publishing books may be ordered through booksellers or by contacting:

Archway Publishing
1663 Liberty Drive
Bloomington, IN 47403
www.archwaypublishing.com
1 (888) 242-5904

Photography by Sabrina Thompson.

ISBN: 978-1-4808-2868-1 (sc)
ISBN: 978-1-4808-2869-8 (hc)
ISBN: 978-1-4808-2867-4 (e)

Print information available on the last page.

Archway Publishing rev. date: 4/22/2016

Dedication

This book is for every girl and every woman who ever thought or felt there were limits to their dreams. To the mothers, whose main goal is to help her daughter realize the greatness within her. I especially dedicate this book to my daughter Jayda who has reignited art and purpose in my life! I love you!

To the beautiful women with the middle name Ann, I honor you. To my mother, Alonia, for making it her purpose to ensure that I knew who and whose I was. To her mother, Beverly, whose artistry, creativity and struggle fuels my work. To her mother Bernyce who embodied love in an agape kind of way. To her mother, Tillie Kay, who I believe prayed prayers that have impacted and kept each generation. If only my life can create a combination of impact in my daughter's life that you have created in mine. And to my friend, Atiya that helped me realize how important this message was for little brown girls. And to her daughter, Bella, whose name means beauty. Baby Girl, I can't wait to see what you do!

To my father Miguel who was taken too soon. Your entrepreneurial spirit lives on in me. To my grandfather Alphonse who showered me in love. To my daddy, the amazing man of God who saw fit to call me his own. And to my wonderful husband, partner and friend, Anthony, I love you. Each of you has inspired who this brown girl is and the woman she has become.

Daneýa

This book is dedicated to every brown girl who wraps sheets and towels around her head and swings back imaginary hair imitating someone else. This is for every brown girl who plays a sport populated by others unlike her. You are fearless. You are loved. You are noticed. For every brown girl hiding in the shadows, I see you.

To Bella Noelle Chase, mommy's Took Nook, you amaze me every day with your radiant personality and "never back down" attitude Your light brightens a thousand nights. You are my inspiration.

To my nieces, Amaya, Sadayah, and Shiloh, glitter and sparkle on!

To my husband, Kenith, for your support on ALL of my MANY endeavors, Elephant Shoes.

To my mother and father, Rwanda and Jeffrey for their love and wisdom, I love you. To my grandmothers, Bessie North and Rose Fisher, for loving the little girl in me before you found rest in Heaven. One day, we will reunite. I love you both.

Atiya

Acknowledgements

We would like to thank our families for their continued support of everything that we do individually and collectively. Thank you to our husbands who kept us on track with every deadline and budget. Thank you, thank you, thank you to our brilliant photographer, Sabrina Thompson, for capturing our vision in each photograph. Your artistry is amazing! Thank you to every parent who believed in this project and trusted us with their little brown beauties. They made this project come alive and to fruition. To our gracious publishing team at Archway Publishing for their support and guidance through this process, thank you!

Whether you are
chocolate, *mocha*, or a
caramel complexion,
Or *round* or *lean*,
plump or *petite*,

Girl, you can
be *anything*!

Whether you have *long* hair, *short* hair, *kinky* hair or *straight*, Girl, you can be *anything*!

Because of your *strengths* in spite of your weaknesses,

Baby Girl, I promise you
can be *anything*.

You are as *tough* as a *tutu*.

You are as *bright* and *cool* as
the bluest of moons.

You were born for this *moment*, born for this *day*.

You were created with a *purpose*
and designed with a *plan.*

You are defined with the *finest* of words.

Lovely, enchanting, amazingly brilliant;
this is who you are.

Your *beauty* is uncompromising.
Your *light* comes from a deep place;

From your mother's, mother's, *mother*.

You are *fearless* and
unapologetically you.

You bring the *poet* out of a sleeping *artist*;

the *color* to a blank canvas.

Songs are written about your *brilliance*.
All along I get to call you *mine*.

Baby, set *ablaze* to the
path that has been laid!

Before the *foundation* of this earth,

You were a *part* of His great big *plan*.

I Love you with the *purist* of loves.

And this village of beautiful
black *kings* and *queens* salute
you as you travel on.

Although *challenges* will come,

Trust that your *purpose* will outweigh any bad day.

There will be plenty of *messages* that tell you that "you can't."

Avoid them.
Ignore them.
They are only *distractions*.

Remember your biggest
competition is *you*.
It is *not* the brown girl
standing next to you.

Practice being your sister's *keeper*, not
just for brown girls but for *all* girls.

Push *forward!*
Never fear *tomorrow.*
You are *safe* in angel's wings.

Forward,
forward,
forward you
will go!

I Love Your Brown

Whether you are chocolate, mocha,
or a caramel complexion,
Or round or lean, plump or petite,
Girl, you can be anything!
Whether you have long hair, short
hair, kinky hair or straight,
Girl, you can be anything!
Because of your strengths in spite of your weaknesses,
Baby Girl, I promise you can be anything.

You are as tough as a tutu.
You are as bright and cool as the bluest of moons.
You were born for this moment,
Born for this day.
You were created with a purpose
and designed with a plan.
You are defined with the finest of words.
Lovely, enchanting, amazingly brilliant;
This is who you are.

Your beauty is uncompromising.
Your light comes from a deep place;
From your mother's, mother's, mother.
You are fearless and unapologetically you.
You bring the poet out of a sleeping artist;
The color to a blank canvas.
Songs are written about your brilliance.
All along I get to call you mine.

Baby, set ablaze to the path that has been laid!
Before the foundation of this earth,
You were a part of His great big plan.
I Love you with the purist of loves.
And this village of beautiful black kings
and queens salute you as you travel on.
Although challenges will come,
Trust that your purpose will outweigh any bad day.
There will be plenty of messages that
tell you that "you can't."
Avoid them. Ignore them. They are only distractions.

Remember your biggest competition is you.
It is not the brown girl standing next to you.
Practice being your sister's keeper, not
just for brown girls but for all girls.
Push forward! Never fear tomorrow.
You are safe in angel's wings.

Forward, forward, forward you will go!

Brown Cutie Guide

As a Brown Cutie, there are so many things about you that are special. Along with an adult, complete your Brown Cutie guide.

My name is _____

When I grow up, I want to be _____

_____

_____

Write down three things you love about yourself.

1. _____

2. _____

3. _____

I am good at _____

_____

_____

One day I hope to change the world by _____

_____

After reading I Love Your Brown, what was your favorite line of the poem? What does this line of the poem mean to you?

_____

_____

_____

There will be days where you do not feel your best. Remember all that you have written down here. These are the things that make you uniquely you. You are loved. You are amazing. You are brilliant. Believe in your brown abilities!

A Mother's Love Letter

With all the negative messages in the world today, a mother's encouraging response to their child's insecurities is like medicine to an open wound. Below, write a love letter to your baby girl. Tell her in your own words how beautiful she is and how much you believe in her. Your love response will drown out the noise and build her brown confidence.

Dear _____,

_____

_____

_____

_____

_____

_____

_____

_____

_____

_____

_____

_____

Love,

_____

Brown Cutie Club
A Call to Action

You are not alone. There are millions of brown girls like you all around the world. They need inspiration, encouragement, and to be celebrated. Let us celebrate you! Grab a parent and a camera. Ask your parent to take a few photos of you and post your favorite one to our Facebook page, I Love Your Brown. Don't forget to tell us all about yourself (your name, age, what you love about yourself and your strengths). Remember, confidence can come from your brown abilities too. Those are most important and will help you to shine bright in the world. You matter, Cutie!

Place your photo here.

WE LOVE YOUR BROWN!

About the Authors

Daneýa L. Jacobs founded Just BE to educate girls about harmful media influences and provide them with tools to create new, uplifting messages of their own. Daneýa lives with her family in Middletown, Delaware.

Atiya Chase holds a Master's in education from Wilmington University and published her first book in 2015. Atiya lives with her family in Townsend, Delaware.

CPSIA information can be obtained
at www.ICGtesting.com
Printed in the USA
LVOW05s0140080317

526423LV00040B/316/P